12.95

IN THE MIDDLE

Cape Dorset

HUDSON STRAIT

scale of miles

0   100   200

LABRADOR SEA

Ivujivik
Saglouc

Bellin

Akulivik

NEWFOUNDLAND

Povungnituk

Fort Chimo

HUDSON BAY

Inoucdjouac

LABRADOR

Belcher Islands

Great Whale

N
W E
S

Fort
George

QUEBEC

Moosonee

ONTARIO

NEW
BRUNS'
WICK

Timmins

Quebec

MAINE

Montreal

Ottawa

ᐊᑯᓐᓂᖓ

IN THE MIDDLE

QITINGANITUK

THE INUIT TODAY

STEPHEN GUION WILLIAMS

INTRODUCTION BY EDMUND CARPENTER

FITZHENRY & WHITESIDE
TORONTO ▸ OTTAWA ▸ WINNIPEG ▸ VANCOUVER

First published in 1983 by
David R. Godine, Publisher, Inc.
306 Dartmouth Street
Boston, Massachusetts 02116

Fitzhenry & Whiteside, Ltd.
150 Lesmill Road
Don Mills, Ontario M3B 2T5
CANADA

Library of Congress Cataloging in Publication Data

Williams, Stephen Guion.
   In the Middle
   Bibliography: p.
   ISBN 0-88902-737-4   1. Inuit—James Bay region (Ont. and Quebec)—
   Social conditions.*   2. Inuit—James Bay region
   (Ont. and Quebec)—Economic conditions.*   3. Inuit—
   James Bay region (Ont. and Quebec)—Pictorial works.*
   I. Title.

E99.E7W54   971.4′100497   C83-098201-9

ISBN 0-88902-737-4 (hardcover)
ISBN 0-88902-738-2 (paperback)

First edition
Printed in the United States of America

My thanks to friend Charles Kirk, who was respon-
sible for planting the seed for this book and who
shared with me our first trip to the North, to Mary-
belle Meyers and Peter Murdock of La Fédération des
Coopératives du Nouveau Québec, and to Minnie
Gray Watt, whose Inuit translations are an important part of this book.

S.W.

12847

In loving memory of Charles Kirk; and of Davidiluk,
who died in my arms and left me with an image.
It is here in this book.

ᑕᐃᕕᑎᐊᓗᒧᑦ; ᑐᕐᑯᓯᒪᒪᒐᕕᑦ ᑕᓚᑲᓂᑦᓱᑎᒃ ᕐᑭᒪᑎᓪᓱᕐᒐ
ᑕᑯᕚᑦᓴᒥᒃ. ᑕᒐᓂᑐᕐᒃ ᕐᑭᒥᕈᐊᒥ. ᓇᑯᕐᒥᒃ ᑕᑦᓱᒥᕐᒐ
ᐊᐃᑐᓯᒪᒪᒐᕕᕐᒐ.

Preface

My introduction to the Eskimo, or Inuit, as they prefer to be called, came in a film class in college. I have always been impressed with early documentary films, especially Robert Flaherty's work. Even though some of the scenes in his films are obviously contrived, they still communicate strong, intimate human feelings. It occurred to me that Flaherty was more concerned with the individual than were most documentary film-makers of his time. In *Nanook of the North*, the Inuit speak for themselves, and their presence is moving and impossible to forget. For days after watching the movie, I played back certain scenes in my mind's eye. *Nanook* made me see how the camera could be used to explain the lives of people in a way no other medium could.

In 1975, through insistence and help from a long-time friend, Charlie Kirk, my interest in the Inuit people was once again piqued. At his suggestion, I began searching for funding for a trip to the Arctic, which led to an assignment from La Fédération des Coopératives du Nouveau Québec to photograph certain Inuit stonecarvers in the eastern coastal villages in that Canadian province.

From my initial contact in that first village, Povungnituk, I was aware of the extreme conflict between past and present in the life of the Inuit. For thousands of years, these people at the top of the world remained remarkably unchanged. Their environment provided them with protection from the ever-expanding white man's world. The last twenty-five years, though, have brought both technical and industrial change to the Arctic. The Inuit are now in transition; they cannot go back — nor are they sure they want to — but they also resist the ways of contemporary man. The conflict between tradition and social assimilation produces an almost schizophrenic way of life. The Inuit live, in a sense, directly in between their two worlds.

Even the Inuit's traditional nomadic habits have been influenced by this split. Always on the move, to hunt or to visit between villages, the Inuit now arrive at these destinations on snowmobiles; they live in unheated canvas tents, but tents outfitted with stereos, mattresses, clocks and the inevitable comic books. They prefer to eat their food raw, but children and young adults now supplement their diet with gum, crackers and soda pop. The change is both subtle and obvious. The Inuit live with one foot in the past and one in the ever-encroaching present. I am always reminded, for example, of the story of the hunter, Peter Adaluk from Ivujivik ('place where ice breaks'), who went hunting on his snowmobile for polar bear, only to run out of gas. He tracked Nanook the remaining distance by foot. After the kill he calmly waited for a passing hunter to give his vehicle a refill; he finally returned to the village three days later. He didn't starve, get lost or freeze to death, and remained the provider for his family.

So what you are seeing in this book is a society in flux. Leaving one well-defined way of life and accepting certain values in another means that huge chunks of the past are thrown out and eventually become unrecognizable to the younger generation. This conflict between new and old becomes a very real struggle for both individual and cultural identity. The process of assimilation unfortunately leaves little visible evidence of what once was. To me this impending loss is overwhelmingly sad, and it became the compelling reason for making these photographs. I just do not want an empty feeling in my stomach because no one was there with a camera.

And to Maggie, Simon and Moses who quietly and patiently shared their lives with me; the memory of that fogbound evening on the island with the men fishing and the women in prayer is still with me.

Stephen Williams
Philadelphia, 1982

Introduction

Who controls the past
controls the future;
who controls the present
controls the past.
ORWELL

These are puzzling photographs. No fur-clad hunters wait for seals; no grandmothers tend igloo lamps; no dog-sleds glide through arctic wastes. Yet we call these people 'Eskimos.'

What does the word mean? Etymologically, it comes from the Algonkian word for 'eaters of raw meat.' Something of that harsh image survives in Western usage. There is, it seems, nothing for us to learn from them, except how to starve on a few fish or build snow-blocks into a shelter.

Yet we should not be too sure. I lived with the Inuit, closely, and often wondered if their myths didn't hold more intense passions, more profound truths, than our most learned talk; whether we might not yet sit at the feet of arctic bards and see shamans enter the kingdom of man before us.

The snow-huts and oil-lamps, dog-sleds and fur-parkas, are gone. 'Inuit' now lies within. This attitude of mind and shape of heart, once in harmony with the community as a whole, past and present, survive today divorced from life, no more than a watch ticking in the pocket of a dead man.

But what is old does not always die, and ideas that once had the power to be considered indisputable truths can rise again, even in an alien setting.

Changes in Eskimo life were, at first, gradual, regional, sometimes temporary. Until the construction of the Defence Early Warning Line in 1955, the forebears of the people photographed here lived in an ancient manner. The web of custom and kinship, with its double strands of marriage and blood, knit together in effective cooperation every person in the group from birth to death.

Then, suddenly and powerfully, came the massive intrusion of western culture, with results so inevitable they can only be charged to the blind forces of history. The new-comers could not see the patterns of Inuit life; they smashed into them almost as innocently as men walk through cobwebs. And so the Inuit lost all of those essential, invisible qualities that give people unity, confidence and self-respect – qualities embedded in patterns, so hard to restore, of a disciplined social life. In return, they were offered, as higher substitutes, free enterprise and Christianity, which few aspired to, and fewer still achieved. The rest were left with material goods and medicine, entertainment and alcohol, and a bitter sense of having lost some indefinable but precious thing.

In the past, everything of value in Inuit life lay within tradition. *Tradition* simply means 'what is transmitted.' What the Inuit transmitted was a way of life, structured in language, expressed in myth, illustrated in art. This metaphysical system wasn't a philosophy in any western sense, but a symmetry of silent assumptions, conceived as perennial, therefore eternal and immutable. No proofs were offered.

I'm reminded equally of *Doxology*: 'As it was in the beginning, is now and ever shall be. World without End;' Augustine: 'Wisdom uncreated, the same now as it was and ever will be;' Lyell: 'Geological processes operating today, operated in the past and will continue to operate in the future.'

What was revealed in the beginning, in Inuit myth, contained explicitly the whole truth. As long as that truth was transmitted faithfully from mothers to daughters, fathers to sons, no room for error existed and life went on.

Renewal was largely rote, yet not always. Understanding refreshened. A statement here, a carving there, stood out. Someone understood.

I met such a man in Ohnainewk, an Aivilik hunter who revealed a glimpse of Inuit life to me. Later I rediscovered that same world in the writings of Knud Rasmussen. I had earlier read Rasmussen, carefully, but only through Ohnainewk did I come to understand those writings. Why this should be, I cannot say, but there's always mystery in truth, perhaps most of all when life and art fuse imperceptibly.

Not that Inuit life was opaque. It was as clear as arctic air, its truths revealed to all in myth and art. But the tales and tools that once expressed these truths now lie sealed in books and vaults, far removed from the living Inuit. In their place, journalists and bureaucrats substituted false equivalents. These are dangerous deceivers. They censor genuine history, replacing it with spurious history.

The Inuit learned genuine history from their own bards, in their own language. Elders told them who they were, where they came from, where value lay. Inuit listened to Inuit.

Spurious history now reaches them through mass media, in scripts written by their conquerors. Journalists and propagandists depict the Inuit as simple in mind and heart, happy in a land of adversity. This benign parading of captives in exotic costumes is made sadder by Inuit acceptance, for these images reach them with all the power and prestige mass media everywhere enjoy, and no alternatives are offered.

Stephen Williams quotes an Inuit's poignant regret that the word *Inukshuk* (person-image) is fading from the language and that stone monuments known as *Inukshuk* no longer resemble people. That quotation is doubly poignant, for in the past these directional markers and hunting sentinels were neither explicitly anthropomorphic nor usually called *Inukshuk*. They acquired both attributes under western guidance: suddenly figures with arms and heads appeared in photographs and at Toronto's airport. When fake becomes genuine, genuine becomes fake.

'The first step in liquidating a people,' said the Czech historian Milan Hubl, 'is to erase its memory. Destroy its books, its culture, its history. Then have somebody write new books, manufacture a new culture, invent a new history. Before long the nation will begin to forget what it is and what it was. The world around will forget even faster.'

My hope is that the Inuit seek out their past, not to imitate some lost ideal, but to realize how who they were, made them what they are. When I'm in search of *me*, I don't want someone else's history. Rejecting your own history means rejecting yourself.

The Inuit who discover their lost heritage may like what they find. In their past lies a record of creative freedom. If awareness of that can be achieved in one or two minds and afterwards in many, creative energies might again be released. History, writes Stephen Gilman, is an arena in which the human condition 'scrutinizes itself and from its anguish recreates in ever original form its sustaining values.'

◄ ◄ ◄

What conditions gave rise to those glorious ivory carvings that appear and reappear in Inuit prehistory? Challenge was surely a factor. It underlay all traditional Inuit life; the goal was perfection. Challenge is the final explanation of Inuit workmanship, of what we call its 'beauty,' despite the fact that the Inuit language has no such term.

Perfection extended to all things. The harpoon was deadly, yet graceful. Grace honored the beast taken. Many carvings were highly intricate. Some were remarkably small.

I know of one so minute only optical magnification discloses a figure holding a child on its shoulders. The carver didn't need to make it that small, didn't need to make it at all — unless challenge be counted necessity.

One might suppose this land challenge enough, but the Inuit constantly challenged themselves. Ohnainewk boasted of putting his rifle aside to confront a bear spear-in-hand. He urged me to attempt it. I thought his suggestion mere bravado. Later I wondered if this attitude wasn't a necessary condition for survival.

Peter Freuchen, the arctic explorer, tells of Inuit parents watching children sliding down an icy slope that ended abruptly at the open sea. It was very dangerous and the faces of the parents betrayed their anxiety, yet no one restrained the children. The Inuit never belittled or degraded anyone who sought to challenge himself, least of all a child.

From birth, a child's dignity was taken for granted. Dignity, the Inuit seemed to be saying, didn't come with age or wealth or wisdom: it was always there; everyone had it, even the youngest. It showed in poised faces, sure hands: people engaged in activities they cared about.

Ohnainewk loved to hunt. He hunted even when food was at hand. He accompanied others when his presence wasn't required. Long after he was too old to hunt, he still wanted to go, as did the youngest boy in camp, who was too small.

The Inuit valued themselves because they valued what they did. When a woman lavished extra care on new boots, then blushingly displayed them, her whole family showed undisguised pride: her husband grinned shamelessly and her children, with no modesty at all, literally filled themselves with air.

Honoring oneself and honoring others were basically the same. What was honored was dignity. An Inuit who felt respected, boasted, no matter how idiosyncratic the achievement. The more challenging that achievement, the more it meant to him — for the same reason we love strong competition in amateur sports: the personal challenge, the joy of commitment. Our amateur athletes pit themselves against the best opponents; mountain-climbers seek the highest peaks. No one pays them and no one needs to watch.

We don't call such effort 'work.' Work we reduce to the short week. We reduce life as well, asking that it be made softer. We protect children from the piercing qualities of living, even from great joys, and particularly from frightening or painful experiences.

But if a thing is worth doing, it's worth being frightened about or suffering for. The Inuit understood this. Toothless Kuilasar told of starvation, of children born and husbands lost, of new lands and faces, and concluded, 'How happy I have been! How good life has been to me!' She hadn't escaped life, nor been rewarded by it, but she had lived fully and that was good.

SEDNA

Of the myths that were once half-told, half-sung in the igloos and sealskin tents, none better illustrates this way of being than the myth of Sedna. Every Inuit knew it and had his own version, all equally true, for this myth was too complex for any single telling.

Sedna or Nuliajuk ('young girl') rejects all suitors until a stranger induces her to elope with him. Actually, he is also a dog, but she discovers this only after reaching her new home on a distant island.

Escape seems impossible until one day her family comes to visit her. Her husband always guards her closely, even ties a long cord to her when she leaves the tent to relieve herself. But this time when she goes outside and he calls, asking why she delays, the cord replies that she will soon return.

In the meantime, she runs to the beach and joins her family in their great walrus-skin boat. But her husband transforms himself into a bird and, swooping low over the boat, turns the sea to storm, threatening them with drowning. To save themselves, they cast Sedna overboard.

At first she clings to the gunwale. But her father cuts off the first joints of her fingers; when she persists, he cuts off the second and third joints. These sink into the sea to become the seal, walrus and whale that Inuit hunt today.

In desperation, Sedna hooks her elbows over the side, but her father strikes her with his paddle, gouging out one eye, and she sinks into the sea, fingerless and one-eyed.

From the bottom of the sea, she now rules all creatures. Their floating bodies nearly fill her house. Periodically she sends these animals forth to be taken by hunters, but only hunters who show respect for slain beasts. Others return empty-handed. That is, Sedna withholds life from them, for they cannot survive without the food, clothing and fuel that come from her offspring.

She is the most feared of all spirits, the one who, more than any other, controls the destinies of men.

In the various versions of this myth, Sedna is sometimes an unwanted daughter cast into the sea by her father, or a girl who has rejected all eligible men, or an orphan nobody wants; in one version, she is already a mother, deserted by her own children. In each, she is someone the family abandons for its own safety.

Abandonment of people was not purely mythical. The Inuit did, in fact, abandon old people. Killing newborn girls was common. And the position of orphans was precarious: one's own family always took precedence. These were normal experiences in Inuit life — cruel necessities forced on them by scarcity.

The Sedna myth represented this dilemma as the Inuit saw it. They never asked that the universe be this way. But, *ayornamut* ('it cannot be otherwise'); they accepted life on its own terms.

They did more than accept: they took upon themselves the responsibility for the fact that life was the way it was. They gave Sedna the power of life and death over them. Those who were forced to abandon her, now placed themselves in her power, dependent upon her good will, her respect for life.

How she exercises that power is revealed in the last part of the myth. A séance takes place in which an *angakok* or shaman tries to save a dying person. He fails, and when the soul goes below to Sedna's house, the *angakok* follows, traveling on the sound of his drum. Sedna's husband, now a dog, blocks the entrance, keeping out the living, keeping in the dead. But the *angakok* paralyzes it with a chant, enters her strange house and confronts her directly. First he tries to reason with her, arguing that she has taken a life without cause. She ignores him. He begs for pity. She laughs. In anger, he twists her arm and beats her with a walrus penis bone. But she is not afraid. Then he becomes cunning and appeals to her vanity by combing out her tangled hair. But she is unrelenting. Finally, ignoring her altogether, he steps back and, with drum held high, sings of life.

Sedna is sometimes so touched by his words, so moved by his singing, she releases the soul of the dead person, allowing it to rejoin the living.

In a land where neither reason nor strength prevail, where cunning counts for little and pity least of all, the Inuit sang of life, for only art prevailed, and even then, not always.

showmanship had cost fifteen lives, but by then the public had discovered Farley Mowat. In a detailed review of Mowat's *People of the Deer*, A. E. Porsild, a distinguished arctic authority, showed that events reported, never occurred; trips described, never happened; people quoted, never lived. In fact, the entire Inuit band whose demise Mowat 'documented,' never existed.

No matter. The book remained a best-seller, quickly followed by another.

What explains such acceptance? Stefansson used the Inuit for self-promotion. He pictured them as capable of many virtues, but only with his help. Their heroism, he suggested, was largely maintained by his own.

Mowat tapped two popular fictions: the Noble Savage and the Noble Victim. No one, of course, really believes in Noble Savages and no one honors victims: we pity them. But both fictions enjoy wide audiences.

The Canadian press, inspired by Mowat's 'reporting,' converted the Inuit from media nonentities into media heroes. At which point the government took over. In the end, it's not romantics who destroy people by their irresponsibility and ignorance, but bureaucrats who translate fiction into propaganda, propaganda into power.

Imaginary Inuit are now ennobled in the media, but the process of grinding real Inuit into a state of living non-existence goes on unchanged. Bureaucrats learned from advertisers how to achieve effects without products.

Central to this propaganda is what passes for 'Eskimo art.' A truly objective study of this souvenir industry would deal with conquest and exploitation, media manipulation and academic corruption.

Profound spiritual and aesthetic differences always divide genuine and spurious art. Perception of these differences is critical to an understanding of both art and people.

Throughout Inuit history, an austere harmony of form and function characterized all tools and weapons. Even when Siberian Metal Age influences prevailed, transforming every object into an elaborate beast, real or mythic, baroque never triumphed. Weapons remained deadly, tools efficient. Siberian art reached its highest expression in arctic America, precisely because of this restraint.

Traditional Inuit art began with function. Hunters designed beautiful weapons to honor beasts of prey, but designs never limited utility. Even ornaments and amulets conformed to the activities of their owners.

Artists carved for challenge, and so for self-esteem. A finished piece might be passed around, examined closely, then used, discarded, lost. Art was an act, not an object.

Today this spirit survives among youths who combine Inuit poetry and rock music, creating art free of alien control. But stonecarvers and printmakers work for money. A recent book on Inuit souvenirs reminds us that Michelangelo worked for money without loss of integrity. Yet he never mass-produced debased Christian altar pieces, suitably modified to meet Arab taste, to peddle on the wharfs of Venice.

Another promotional book quotes Henry Moore: '[primitive art] makes a straight-forward statement, its primary concern is with the elemental, and its simplicity comes from direct and strong feelings . . . the most striking quality common to all primitive art is its intense vitality. It is something made by people with a direct and immediate response to life.'

Such statements are wrong. No matter how naked a people, no matter how tormented their situation, no one lives an 'elemental,' 'simple,' 'direct,' 'immediate' life. People everywhere are pattern-makers and pattern-perceivers; they live in symbolic worlds of their own creation.

Moore's unfortunate choice of words may simply reflect an imperial background. Yet that quotation, in that context, remains troublesome, for the Inuit were trained to make these souvenirs by a Canadian artist who admired Moore to the point of imitation. Inuit souvenirs bear more than a coincidental similarity to Moore's work, a similarity that helps market them.

Calling these western-inspired, government-controlled, mass-produced souvenirs 'art' is absurd and sentimental. It is false to believe art can be divorced from the truth in which it originates, or that the only end of art is to amuse.

'It's the power of belief,' writes Froelich Rainey, 'which makes all the difference between original native art and contemporary native craft.'

The most diverse motives can lie behind art, but without belief and challenge, it's never art, and even these are not enough.

Bill Reid, the Haida carver, wrote to me: 'In the early days of printmaking and soap-stone carving, a few truly gifted individuals accepted the new media as another challenge to be confronted with the same eagerness and courage that they brought to other pursuits. I think they brought in from the ice a fund of genius and delight in accomplishment that far transcended the limited vision of the southern instigators of the new means of ex-pression and for a brief, magical moment let us share something of their view of the world, something of what it is to be the product of those long centuries of fine tuning which enabled them to live such marvelously human lives in such inhuman circumstances. After a quarter of a century, some of these old images are still fresh and vivid in my mind.

'Most of the hundreds of thousands of pieces of "Eskimo art" produced since the 50s is junk, although compared to similar exploitations, it's quite remarkable junk. Imbedded in this rough matrix are an unlikely number of artistic gems and a few masterpieces.'

In the past, a few; today, none. In May, 1982, I visited an 'Eskimo art' gallery in New York: carvings and prints were uniformly depressing; literature and promotion were explicitly dishonest. Subjects and styles didn't derive from the Inuit, but from buyers' fiction and fashions. Clumsy harpoons replaced graceful weapons. A simple stone lamp was so erroneously designed it could never work. And Sedna was everywhere.

In the past, Sedna was rarely depicted and then only as a surreal form, experienced first as an inner vision. Here she was rendered naturalistically, as a mermaid, that sexually inaccessible figure who frustrates mariners. Her hair was combed; her fingers intact; her tale forgotten.

Art and poetry are channels whereby passions reveal themselves. Increasingly this souvenir industry reveals subservience. It's not the art of a free people, but merely a means of exploitation and manipulation.

Of course, the world is full of exploitative charlatans. Those who promote Inuit souvenirs like their primitive art to look primitive, as they appoint themselves high priests of the badly made object, then write bad books and attract a certain following. They may not have been the people I would have chosen to reinvent the arctic, but what happened would have happened anyway.

◄ ◄ ◄

Is there, then, no honest image of the Inuit? After a thousand years of contact, has no European come to know an Inuit as a human being and left an honest record?

Knud Rasmussen left just such a record. To me, his writings compare to those of Homer, Dante, Tolstoy. He lacked their creative powers of language, but all that is human is there, especially dignity. Listen to what Orpingalik told him:

'*My Breath* – this is what I call this song, for it is just as necessary to me to sing as it is to breathe,' and then he began:

I will sing this song
A song that is strong

'Songs,' he added, 'are thoughts, sung out with the breath when people are moved by great forces and ordinary speech no longer suffices. Man is moved just like an ice floe sailing here and there out in the current. His thoughts are driven by a flowing force when he feels joy, when he feels sorrow. Thoughts can wash over him like a flood, making his blood come in gasps and his heart throb. Something, like an abatement in the weather, will keep him thawed up. And then it will happen that we, who always think we are small, will feel still smaller. And we will fear to use words. But it will happen that the words we need will come of themselves. When the words we want to use shoot up of themselves – we get a new song.'

For equally strong images, one turns to Robert Flaherty's film, *Nanook of the North*. Those proud faces will not go out of mind and be forgotten. Everything Flaherty filmed, photographed and wrote reveals the dignity of others, no matter how harsh their lives, no matter how alien their lives from ours.

It comes through, as well, in Stephen Williams' own photographs. Of those charged with witnessing the ordeal of modern Inuit life, few have left so truthful and compassionate a record.

Freedom and dignity didn't reach the Inuit as gifts from outside. Both were already there, expressed in myth and art. But today those tales and tools lie stored in vaults, guarded by strangers. To us has been committed the care of these vast and antique dreams. We study them for the sake of making them part of our imagination.

Inuit involvement has vaster purposes. For them, these ancient arts offer a path to identity.

That path was defined long ago: return to the austere values of the past; draw from within; then ride through the air to the bottom of the night and there, among the dead, surrounded by thronging crowds of angry and malign presences, confront Sedna, cruel patroness, who offers but one felicity: life again to those who sing of life.

Edmund Carpenter
New York, 1982

References and Readings

Knud Rasmussen's best writings appear in the *Reports of the Fifth Thule Expedition, 1921–24*: 7:1, Iglulik Eskimos, 1929; 7:2–3, Caribou Eskimos, 1930; 8:1–2, Netsilik Eskimos, 1931; 9, Copper Eskimos, 1932.

I also recommend Peter Freuchen's novel, *Eskimo*, 1931; as well as Robert Flaherty's *The Story of Comock the Eskimo*, 1968; and *Drawings by Enooesweetok of the Sikosilingmint Tribe, Fox Lane, Baffin Land*, 1915. Flaherty describes the filming of *Nanook of the North* in *My Eskimo Friends*, 1924; as does Frances Hubbard Flaherty in *The Odyssey of a Film-maker*, 1960; and more recently, though with frequent inaccuracy, Jo-Anne Birnie Danzker, Jay Ruby *et al.*, in *Robert Flaherty*, 1980.

Vilhjalmur Stefansson's *The Friendly Arctic*, 1921, is placed in perspective by William Laird McKinlay's *Karluk*, 1977. A. E. Porsild in *The Beaver*, June, 1952, renders the same service with Farley Mowat's *People of the Deer*, 1951. Mowat's most amusing error is his charge that traders drastically reduced caribou herds by encouraging the Inuit to collect caribou tongues – 'caribou tongue' being the Northern term for a plant used to flavor tobacco.

Traditional Inuit art is described by Henry B. Collins, 'Eskimo Cultures,' *Encyclopedia of World Art*, 5, 1962; Jørgen Melgaard, *Eskimo Sculpture*, 1965; and Edmund Carpenter, *Eskimo Realities*, 1973.

For illustrations of souvenir carvings, see George Swinton, *Eskimo Sculpture*, 1965; Cottie Burland, *Eskimo Art*, 1973; Carson I. A. Ritchie, *The Eskimo and His Art*, 1975; and Dorothy Jean Ray, *Eskimo Art*, 1977; as well as various exhibition and promotional catalogs published in Ottawa.

Major collections of traditional arctic art exist (largely in storage) at the national museums in Washington, Ottawa, Copenhagen and Moscow. Most carvings, however, still lie frozen in ancient sites. Today their safety is much endangered by looting. In Alaska, no legislation prohibits such looting, and in Canada, though looting is illegal, authorities actually promote it by marketing Inuit souvenirs made of whale bone torn out of ancient Thule sites.

In the Middle

The Land. A horizontal landscape referred to as the Tundra by geologists. It is known generally as the Arctic, the 'top of the world.' The Inuit call it 'the barrens.'

For me it is like a desertscape transformed into petrified sculpture. Quiet but strong. Restful but alive. And always the feeling that here Nature is still in control.

To live here is to learn. The incremental passage of time becomes insignificant. Only light and darkness prevail. It is the Inuit's world. They feel the rhythm of the Land. They know the animals who live here. And, if you listen, they will tell you of themselves.

ᓄᓇ ᒫᖅᖁᔪᐃᐊᖅ ᓇᐊᖅ ᔭᐊᔭᐳᓄᖅᕿ ᑕᐅᒌᖅ ᓄᐊᑎᐳᓂᐨ.
ᖃᐅᕆᒪᔭᐅᔪᓂᖅᕿ ᐸᒥᐊᖅ ᐅᐱᐅᕿ ᑕᔭᒥ, 'ᒥᐨᕿ ᐨᐊᐨ ᖅᕿᒡ.'
ᐃᓄᑎᐊᓄᐨ ᐊᐨᒥᖅᕿ ᑕᐅᕆᖅ 'ᓄᓇ ᕆᐊᖅᐨᐊᔭᖅᕿ.'

ᐅᐸᓂᐨ ᐃᖅᕿᐊᓇᔭᖅᕿ, ᖁᔭᐧᔨᐨᐧᐊᔭᖅ ᕆᐊᖅᐧᐊᔭᔭᖅᕿ
ᐊᐳᐨᐨᐧᐸᔭᔭᖨᐨᐧᐊᔨᐨ ᕆᓇ ᖃᐧᔪᐧᐧᑕᐨᐧᐧᐊᐧᐊᓄᐅᕿᐨ ᔭᖅ.
ᓄᐸᔭᔪᐨᐧᐧᐨᖅ ᕿᔨᐧᐧᐧᐊᔭᐧᖅ. ᐅᐨᐧᐨᐟ ᖑᐨᕿᐧᖅᐧᖅ ᐅᐨᐧᔪᐧᐧᐊᕿ ᕆᓇ.
ᐧᐧᐧᔪ ᐃᐧᐧᕿᐧᐧᐧᐧᐨᐧᐨ ᕆᐧᐨᐨ ᐧᐨᐧᕿ ᑕᐧᓇ ᐧᐨᐧᔭᔪᐅᐧᐧᔪᐧᐨᕿ.

ᐧᐧᐧᐨ ᕿᖅ ᔪᐧᐨᐧᐧᔪ ᑕᐧᓇ ᐃᐧᐧᐧᐅᐧᔪᐧᐅᐸᔮᖅᕿ. ᕆᖅᐧᔨᖅᐳᐨ ᐅᔪᑕᐧᐳᐅᐨ
ᐧᐨ ᖅᐟᕿ ᐧᐨᐧᐊᔪᐧᔮ ᐃᐧᐸᕆᐊᐃᕆᖅᕿ. ᖃᐅᐅᐧᐅᖅ ᑕᐟ ᕆᐧᐟᕿ ᓄᔪᐧᕆᐧᐧᐊᓄ
ᕆᔭᐧᐨᐅᔭᖅ. ᐃᐧᔪᐃᐧᐊᐃᐨ ᕆᐨᕿ ᐧᐧᔭᕿᒡ. ᓄᐧᐅᐨᐨ ᐧᐃᐳᐨᐧᕿᕿᐨᐅᖅ
ᐃᐧᔭᐃᐧᐧᐳᔭᐨᐨ. ᖃᐅᕆᒪᐧᔪ ᐅᕆᐧᐅᐨ ᑕᐧᓇᐨᐨᐅᐨ. ᐧᐧᔪ,
ᓄᐨᐃᐧᔭᐨᐨ, ᐃᐧᕆᐅᐨ ᐅᐃᕿᐅᐨᕿᐧᐅᐧᔪᐨ ᐃᓄᐅᐨ.

The winter house, traditionally known as the Iglu, has become a two-bedroom heated home. Tivi once remarked, *We never liked the Iglu . . . it was cold. We always wanted to be warm.*

ᐅᏢᐅᒥ ᐃᓄᖅ, ᖃᐅᐱᓚᖑᐅᒍᑎᖅᔆᒪᕐᓚᐊᖅ ᐃᓄᐊᓕᖅᒥᖅ, ᐃᓄᑐᐋᓈᑉᔆᒪᕐᓚᐊᖅ, ᒪᖔᓂᖅ ᖅᑲᐅᐊᖅ ᐅᔆᑐᕐᔆᐳᕐᓂ. ᑎᐱ ᐅᖅᑊᔆᒪᕐᓚᐊᖅ, 'ᐃᓄᐊᓕᖅ ᐊᓕᐊᕐᒪᔆᑕᖅ. . . ᖅᐱᐅᓕᔆᐅᐊᓈᕐᓚᐊᖅ. ᐅᔆᖅᐃᓕᖅᑲᑕᕐᓚᐳᔆ.'

I never liked the winter. It is too dark. It is the summer with the light and long days. . . .

ᶜᏯᕐᏰᏴᐃᐊᖅ ᐊᒐᐊᒋᓕ ᕗᒪᕐᒐᑕ. ᖏᐃᐸᐊᒍᐊᐟ ᐟᐊᒍᖅ.
ᐅᑉᓕᕈ ᖅᑲᐃᒪᕐᐊᑉᖅ ᐊᒪᒍ ᐅᒍᑐᔐᐊᑉᖅ. . . .'

To visit the Inuit in their summer camps is to understand them more. They seem to shed reserve as they return to the Land from their westernized villages. They hunt, they talk, they love, they carve. It is a time for re-entering their past. And for the visitor, a glimpse at what once was.

ᐳᓚᕆᐊᕐ ᑕᐅᒐᒥᒃ ᐃᓄᑐᐃᓇᐃᑦ ᐊᐅᓛᓯᒪᕕᒥᓂᑎᑐᕆᑦ ᐅᐱᕐ ᖓᑯᑦ ᑐᑭᓯᓚᐅᒥᒥᐊᓚᓇᕐ ᑐᑦ. ᑲᑦ ᓱᖓᓂᕐ ᒥᒃ ᑲᑕᒐᐃᔪᔭᕐ ᑐᑦ ᓄᓇᒧᑦ ᐅᑎᓚᕿᒥᒃ, ᓄᓇᓕᒥᓂᑦ ᖃᓗᓇᓕᕐ ᑕᒥᑦ ᐱᑦ ᓱᑎᒃ. ᐅᒪᔪᕐ ᓯᐅᑐᕐ, ᐅᖃᔪᑦ, ᓇᓕᒍᓱᑐᑦ, ᓴᓇᕐᒍᐊᑐᑦ. ᑕᐃᑦ ᓱᒪᓂᑕᕕᓂᕐ ᒧᑦ ᐅᑎᕐ ᓇᓯᐅᓯᒥᔪᑦ. ᐊᒪᓗ ᑕᓇ ᐳᓚᕐ ᑐᖅ, ᓯᑯᕐᕆᓚᓂᐊᐱᐅᔭᕐ ᑐᑯᑦ ᑕᑯᕗᖅ, ᐱᐅᓯᐅᓚᐅᕐ ᑐᕕᓂᕐ ᒥᒃ.

The tents. Like frozen sculpture they stand against the wind tethered by rock; nomads in these barren plains. They are from another time, another place. Now, they remain as a symbol of resistance to the ever-quickening pace of the new world.

ᑐᐱᑦ. ᖂᐊᖅ ᑎᒍᑦ ᓴᓇᔪᐊᕈᓚᐅᖅᓯ ᑐᑦ ᒪᑕᒐᔨᑦ ᐊᓗᑎᒥ
ᐱᐢᕐ ᑐᓲᓚᑦ ᓯᑎᖅ ᐅᖅᖁᖅ ᓄᑦ; ᐃᓄᑦ ᓴᐃᐊᒥᓄᐊᔪᑦ ᓇᐸᖅ ᑐᐊᑐᐸ
ᓇᑎᖅ ᓇᕐᓂ. ᐊᕈᐊᓄᑦ ᐱᐅᕐᖅ ᒥ, ᐊᕈᐊᓄᓪ ᐃᓂᕐ ᑦ
ᐱᕈᓚᐈᑦ. ᓚᓇᓗ, ᐅᐃᑕᑎᑦ ᕐᔪᓂᐅᖅᓄᖅ ᖅᑦ ᕺᓚᐅᑦ ᑕᐃᓂᓇᖅ ᒥᐸ
ᑕᒪᑦ ᕐᔪᓪ ᐅᐱᒪᓄᐊᔪᖅᑰᐊᒧᑦ ᓄᑦ ᕐᓂᖅ ᕐᐊᐢ.

The Inuit communicate now between their summer camps with shortwave radio and satellite. Soon, there will be telephones and finally television.

ᐃᓄᑐᐃᓇᐃᑦ ᑐᖅᑲᑕᐅᑎᒐᓂᕐᔪᒡᔪᑦ ᐊᐅᒡᕆᒪᖃᑎᒐᕂᓐᖅ
ᓇᑲᑎᐊᐱᑎᒍᑦ ᐊᒡᓗ ᐳᒐᑕᐃᒡᐳᑎᒍᑦ. ᒪᕂᑎᐳᑎᒑᐱᖅ
ᑕᓗᕕᖕᖅ ᐅᖅᑲᑎᖕᖃᔾᒍᓐᑕᕂᑐᑦ ᐊᒡᓗ ᑕᑲᐱᕂᖅ.

The Inuit

Solomonie Alayko; his story was one of the first I was told. One day in the Fall he decided he would walk with his sled to the next village, five days distant, to see his girlfriend, Laliemi. He did this. They married and spent their honey-moon on the way back to Akulivik ('between the two'). They are there now, and when I talked to Solomonie Alayko they had just seen their son off on his Ski-doo to fetch his wife. I later heard that he had got lost.

ᓴᓚᒧᓂ ᐊᓚᑯ; ᐅᓂᑲᐅᓯᕐᒐ ᑐᓴᑎᐊᕐᒐᓯᒪᔭᑲᓄᑦ ᓯᕗᓕᐸᐅᕐᑲᑕᐅᓯᒪᔪᕐᒃ.
ᐅᑭᐊᕐᒍᑎᓗᒍᒍᕐᒃ ᐱᓱᓯᔭᕕᓂᕐᒃ ᕐᑲᒧᑎᓕᔭᕐᓱᓂ ᓄᓇᓕᐅᑉ ᐊᐃᐸᓄᑦ,
ᑕᓕᒪᓂᒃ ᐅᓗᓂᒃ ᐱᓱᒥᐊᓕᒍᑦ, ᓂᕐᒥᐅᓱᒥᓂᒃ ᓚᓕᒥᒃ ᑕᑯᓂᐊᓯᑦᓱᓂ.
ᑕᐃᒪᐃᓕᓂᕆᒥ, ᑳᑎᑕᐅᔭᕕᓂᒃ ᑳᑎᑕᐅᕐᑲᒥᐅᓂᕐᒥᓂ ᐊᑯᓕᕕᓕᐊᓕᕐᑐᕕᓂᒃ.
ᑕᐃᑲᓂᒥᐅᕐᒍᕗᑕᒐ, ᐊᒪᓗ ᐅᕐᑲᕐᑲᑎᕆᔭᕆᓂ ᓴᓚᒧᓂ ᐊᓚᑯ, ᐃᕐ ᓂᒥᓂᒃ
ᐊᐅᓚᕆᑕᕐ ᓂᕆᐃᓚᐅᕐ ᓯᒪᔪᕐᒃ ᐊᕐ ᓇᒥᓂᒍᕐᒃ ᓯᑭᑐᑯᑦ ᐊᐃᓯᓯᔭᒥᒃ.
ᐊᑯᓂᐅᓕᕐᒪᑦ ᑐᓴᓕᓚᐅᕐ ᓯᒪᕗᕐᒐ ᐊᓯᐅᔭᕕᓂᐅᒥᐊᕐᒐᓂᒃ.

My mother taught me how to skin the fish and prepare it for my family. . . . I am thirteen. Soon I will be married and have children and go riding on my husband's snowmobile and go to the dance and movie on Saturday nights. My grandfather does not talk anymore about when he was my age.

ᑊᐊᓇᓇᒪᓄᑦ ᐃᓕᓂᐊᑎᑕᐅᓯᒪᒍᕐᒐ ᐃᖅᑲᓗᓕᕆᒥᐊᒥᒃ ᐊᒪᓗ ᐊᑐᐃᓇᕈᖅ ᑎᓯᒍ ᐃᓚᒪ ᓂᕆᓚᕐᒐᔪᕐᒐ. . . . ᖁᓕᓗ ᐱᕐᒐᓯᓗᓂᒃ ᐅᑭᐅᖅᑲᖅ ᑐᕐᒐ. ᒪᓇᑲᓴᒃ ᐊᕐᒍᑎᑕᑦᓴᐅᑎᒥᓚᖅ ᑐᕐᒐ ᐊᒪᓗ ᐱᐊᖅᑭᐅᓯᓗᕐᒐ, ᐊᕐᒍᑎᒪ ᓯᑭᑐᕐᒪᓂ ᐊᑐᖅᑲᑕᓗᕐᒐ ᐊᒪᓗ ᐊᓚᕐᒥᓱᕐᒪᐅᓕᑐᐊᖅ ᐸᑦ ᑕᒃ ᖄᓕᔭᕆᐊᖅ ᐸᓗᕐᒐ ᑕᓂᓯᕆᐊᖅ ᑐᐸᓗᕐᒪᓗ. ᐊᑕᑕᑦ ᓯᐊᖁ ᐅᓂᑲᖅᑲᔪᕈᓇᐃᑐᖅ ᑕᐃᑦ ᓯᒪᓂ ᐅᕙᓂᒃ ᑕᐃᒪᐃᑯᐊᖅᑲᖅ ᓯᓂ ᐱᐅᓯᕖᓂᖅ ᒥ ᒥᑦᓴᓄᑦ.

Tomassie makes a kayak for the museum. His grandchildren play in the sun while he patiently carves and fits the pieces together. They are from the wood of abandoned snowmobile crates.

When I showed this photograph to Tomassie's grandchildren, they asked me what it was. I explained. They nodded and replied that they had heard it mentioned in one of his stories.

ᑐᒪᓯ ᖃᔭᖅᐅᐱᔅ ᑐᖅ ᑕᐃᑦ ᓯᓗᓂᑳᑯᐱᒥ ᑕᑐᐂᖃᐃᖓᖅ. ᐃᔅ ᔪᑕᖃᑉᖃ ᓯᖁᓇᑐᐊᐱᒥ ᐱᒍᐊᑐᖅ, ᓇ ᑐᒪᓯ ᐅᐱᒪᒍ ᓇᐅᑭᓱᓱ ᐊᖁᕐᐊᖅ ᕐᓇ ᖃᔭᖃᖓᖅ. ᑕᑯᐊ ᖁᐊᖁᖅ ᖃᔭᖃᐊᖓᖅ ᕐᑉ ᐃᖅ ᖃᖏᒐᓂᖅ ᕐᖃ ᕐᐊᓂᖃᖅ.

ᓇ ᐊᖅ ᑉᔪᐊᖃ ᑕᑯᓴᐅᓇᖃᑐ ᑐᒪᓯᐅ ᐃᔅ ᔪᖃᒥᓱ, ᐊᐱᓇᓐᑐ ᕐᓇᐅᒪᑉ. ᑐᖅᓇᓐᑐᐊᕐᖃ. ᐊᖏᓇᖅ ᖃᐂᓇᑐᐊᖅ ᑐᖅᖃᖃᓄᕐᖅ ᕐᓐᖅ ᑕᖅ ᕐᒥᒪ ᐊᑕᖅᖁᐊᒥ ᐅᓇᖏᖃᓇ.

Simon Aliqu. Hunter, shaman, father. He belongs to both
worlds, the former and the present. He travels between them.
But there is pain in his eyes and silence in his speech.
He knows what has been lost and now what must be.

ᓯᐊᒪ ᐊᓚᒍ. ᒫᖃᐱᑎ, ᐊᙱᒐᖅ, ᐊᑖᖅ. ᑕᒫᕆᓄᓚᒃᕿᖅ
ᓯᓂᔅ ᐁᐊᓄᑦ, ᓯᐅᑲᐱᓂᔅ ᒍᑦ ᐊᓗ ᒪᓄᐅᓂᔅ ᑐᒍᑦ. ᐊᑯᓂᑯ
ᐊᔅ ᐁᑕᔅ ᐸᑐᖅ. ᐱᓄᐊᓄ ᐊᓄᐊᑕᕿ ᐃᓄᑎᖅ ᐊᓗ ᐅᖅᐅᓄᔅᑕ
ᓄᐸᐊᑐᖅ. ᖃᐅᐸᒪᕿ ᓵᓇᐃᔅ ᐊᓕᐅᓕᒪᑕᑕ ᐊᓗ ᒪᓇ
ᖃᓄᐁᑦᓗᓂᐅᑎᐊᖅᐸᓯ ᒪᔅᒪᔅ.

Inside

Adamee once told me that *inside . . . I can re-enter our world. It is quiet and I can dream. It is as if I am suspended in time; I remain between the past and future.*

ᐊᑕᒥ ᒍᑦ ᐅᖃᐅᓯᐅᐸᓚᐅᑦ ᓯᒪᕆᖅᒥ 'ᐃᓗᖓ. . . ᐅᑎᕐ ᓴᐊᓇᖃᓇᖅᒥ ᓯᓚᖅ ᑕᐊᑎᓄᑦ. ᓂᐸᐃᑐᖅ ᐊᓗ ᓯᐊᑐᒪᓇᑐᖅᒥ. ᖃᐃᑕᑦᕐᓗᖅ ᑐᖅᒥ ᑕᒪᑐᐃᓇᖅ; ᖁᑎᖑᓄᑦ ᓱᖅᒥ ᑕᐃᑦ ᓯᓗᓇᑕᐅᕐ ᐊᓗ ᓯᖂᓇᑦ.'

The men are hunting, children either playing or in school.
Outside it is a sharp, fiercely cold day. Inside Maggie is alone
. . . with herself. For a moment as she sits I catch a glimpse
of quiet determination. And then it's gone, but she has given
me something of herself. I nod in appreciation.

ᐊᕐᓇᑦ ᒪᖅᐳᑦ, ᐱᐊᕋᐃᑦ ᐱᒍᐊᑐᑦ ᐅᖃᓄᑦ ᐃᓄᕐᐊᑐᑦ.
ᓯᒥ ᐃᑦᐳᓚᑦ ᑐᒪᕐᐊᑐᓪ ᓇᓂᓂᒐᑦ, ᖅᑯᐳᖁᑦ ᑐᕐᖅ. ᐃᒍ ᐃᑦᐊᓂ
ᒪᑭ ᐃᒪᑐᐊᖅᑦ. . ᐃᒥᓂᖅᕕᖅ. ᐊᑯᓂᐅᑦᒐᐊᐊᐱᓗᐊᒪ
ᑕᓇ ᒪᑭ ᐃᑦ ᕈᐸᑕᓕᑦ ᑎᓘᑐᑦ, ᕈᖅᖏᑕᓄᐊᐊᕕᖅ ᑐᖅᑦ ᑕᖁᖅᒥᒪ
ᓄᐸᐃᑐᓗᐊᖅᑦ ᕐᐊ ᑲᕐᕈᑦᐸᐃᓗᒥᓯᓄᖅ. ᐊᕐᐃᑕ ᑕᓗᐊᒪ
ᑕᖁᒥᑫ ᐊᕈᐅᑎᑦ ᖅᑦ, ᕈᕐᐊᓂ ᐊᒥᓂᑦᒥᖅ ᐅᖃᓄᑦ ᓄᐃᑦ ᕈᒍᖅᑦ.
ᓄᐊᑐᒐᓂᑦ ᐊᑦᓘᒥ ᐊᑐᑦ ᒥᕐᐅ.

Simon and Maggie Aliqu. A family caught in the middle. There are seven children: Nellie, Moses, Timothy, Annie, Peter, Simeonie, and Elizabeth. They were the first family to move back to Cape Smith (Akulivik) from the larger village Povungnituk. Simon had left the Cape as a boy, when the sickness (tuberculosis) destroyed most of its people. Now he has returned in an attempt to separate his family, to keep them from being absorbed too fast. But they have been pursued by time and it has caught up to them. Still, they exist as a family. Simon told me once that soon they will move again.

ᓴᐃᒪ ᐊᒪᓗ ᒪᑭ ᐊᓚᑯ. ᐃᓚᒋᕐᒍᔪᒃ ᐊᑯᓂᕐᒐᓂᒥᐅᑕᒃ. ᓯᑕᒪᐅᔪᕐᒋᒐᕐ ᑐᓂᒃ ᕿᑐᖕᒐᓕᒃ; ᓂᐊᓕᒥ, ᒧᓯᓯᒥᒃ, ᑎᒧᑎᒥᒃ, ᐊᓂᒥᒃ, ᐱᑕᒥ, ᓯᒥᐅᓂᒥᒃ ᐊᒪᓗ ᐃᓕᓴᐱᒥᒃ. ᓯᕗᓕᐸᐅᑦᓯᑎᒃ ᐅᑎᕆᐊᕐᒐᓯᔪᕕᓂᒃ ᐊᑯᓕᕕᒧᑦ ᐳᕕᕐ ᓂᑐᒥᑦ. ᑕᓇ ᓴᐃᒪ ᓱᕈᓯᐊᐱᐅᑦ ᓱᓂᓱᓕ ᕿᒪᐃᓚᐅᕐ ᑐᕕᓂᖅ ᐊᑯᓕᕕᒥᒃ, ᐊᓂᐊᒧᑦ ᐳᕈᓗᓇᕐ ᒧᑦ ᐃᓄᕐᒋᑦ ᑐᕐᑯᕋᕐ ᑐᐊᓗᓕᕐᒪᑕ. ᑕᒪ ᐅᑎᕐ ᓯᒪᓕᕆᕗᖅ ᐃᓚᒥᓂᒃ ᐊᓯᐊᒍᕐ ᑎᓯᒥᐊᕈᒪᑦ ᓱᓂ, ᓱᑲᓗᐊᕐ ᑐᒥᒃ ᓄᓱᑕᐅᕐᑯᓇᒋᑦ. ᑭᓯᐊᓂ ᐅᓚᑕᐅᒐᒥᒃ ᐱᕈᓕᐊᓂᕐ ᒧᑦ ᐊᕐᒍᑎᔭᐅᑐᐃᓇᕐᑯᑦ. ᕋᓗᐊᕐ ᓱᑎᒃ, ᐃᓚᒋᓂᒥᒍᑦ ᓄᐃᑕᕐᒋᓇᑐᑦ. ᓴᐃᒪ ᑕᓇ ᐅᕈᓄᑦ ᐅᕐᑲᓚᐅᕐ ᓯᒪᔪᖅ ᒪᓇᒃᓴᑯᑦ ᓄᒋᐊᓕᕋᔭᕐ ᓂᕋᕐ ᓱᓂ.

Stonecarvers

The stonecarvers' tent: separate, apart, alone. Inside the men recreate their dreams from stone. These are the legends the white man buys.

Once I watched for three days a man with his piece of soapstone. As the hours passed and shapes became apparent, I understood what one Inuit said: *First you must feel the Spirit of the Stone. It will tell you what to say. Then your friendship begins.*

ᐅᔭᕋᕐᒥᒃ ᓴᓇᕐᒍᐊᑎᐅᑉ ᑐᐱᕐᒐ: ᐊᕕᐅᓯᒪᕙᖅ; ᐃᒥᒍᕐ ᑐᖅ, ᐃᓱᑐᐊᖅ. ᐃᓗᐊᓂ ᐊᕐᒍᑎᑦ ᓴᓇᕙᑦ ᓯᓇᑐᒪᕆᓕᓂᕐ ᒥᓂᒃ ᐅᔭᕋᕐ ᒧᔭᕐ ᓱᕆᑦ. ᑕᑯᐊᑕᒐ ᐅᓂᑲᑐᐊᑦ ᖃᓗᓇᑦ ᓂᐅᕕᕐ ᐸᑕᕐᕆᑦ.

ᑕᑯᓇᓚᐅᕐ ᓯᒪᒥᒐᒪ ᐊᕐᒍᑎᒥᒃ ᖁᓕᓴᔭᒥᒃ ᓴᓇᕙᒥᒃ ᐱᕐᒐᓱᓂ ᐅᑐᓂ. ᑲᐃᕙᓚᒍᓯᑦ ᖃᕐᕆᕐ ᐸᓕᐊᓂᕐᒐᓄᑦ ᐊᒪᓗ ᓴᓇᔭᕐᒐᑕ ᑐᑭᑕᕐ ᐸᓕᐊᓂᕐᒐᓄᑦ, ᑐᑭᓯᓕᓚᐅᕐ ᓯᒪᒐᕐᒐ ᐃᓄᑐᐃᓇᐅᑉ ᐅᖃᕐ ᓯᒪᔭᕐᒐᓂᒃ: 'ᓯᕗᓕᐸᒥ ᑕᑦ ᓱᒪ ᐅᔭᕋᐅᑉ ᐊᓂᕐ ᓂᑯᑦ ᑕᕐ ᓂᐅᔭᕐᒐ ᐃᐱᕆᖃᕆᐊᓕᒃ. ᖃᐅᔨᑦ ᓯᓚᕐᒐᕙᖅ ᖃᓄᐃᓕᕆᐊ-ᖃᕐ ᒪᕐᒐᐱᑦ. ᐊᓱᐃᓚ ᐃᓚᓇᕆᓂᑎᒃ ᐱᕆᐊᕐ ᓂᐊᓕᕐ ᒪᑦ.'

There are two men fighting. They are both Inuit. One is the first and the other the last Eskimo. I don't know who will be the one to die first.

ᒻᒃ ᖃᓄᒃ ᐊᔾᔨᓄᒃ ᐸᑦᑕᖕ. ᐃᓄᑐᐃᓐᐊᐅᖅᑭᑎᕆᒃ. ᐊᐃᖃᒻ
ᐃᓄᑐᐃᓐᐊᐅᑏᐊᒡᒥᔪᒪᑦᖅ ᐊᒡᓗ ᐊᐃᖃᒻ ᐃᓄᑐᐃᓐᐊᓐᒡᐃᑦᐱᐱᑕᕆᖅ ᑐᖅ.
ᖅᐅᖅᒪᒡᑐᒡᒃ ᐊᓴᐊ ᑐᒡᖅᑲᓂᖅ ᓴᐱᓴᐊᖅ ᒪᒡᒥᑕᖅ.'

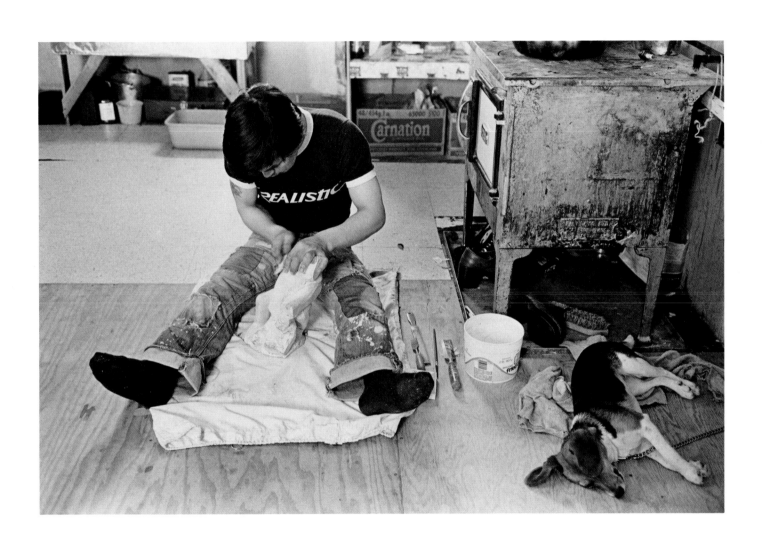

Hunting

Beast of the Sea
Come offer yourself in the dear early morning!

Beast of the Plain
Come offer yourself in the dear early morning!

The Inuit are the only hunting culture left on the North
American continent.

On the Northwestern Coast they hunt the great bowhead
whale and on the Eastern Coast the seal, caribou, and
Nanook, the polar bear.

Hunting is still, and always has been, precious to them. So
is the sharing of food. Their understanding of the Land and
the Animal is an intimate one, and it is important to them
that these two things still affect their being.

ᐃᓄᑐᐃᓇᐃᑦ ᐅᒪᔨᕐ ᓯᐅᐅᓂᕐᒥᖅ ᐃᑦᔪᕐᖅᑉᕐ ᓱᑎᖅ ᐊᒥᐊᒃᑐᕐᕐ ᑐᐨ
ᑕᓗ ᑲᓇᑕᐅᑉ ᓄᐊᕐ ᐸᑎᑦᒍ.

ᑕᓗ ᑲᓇᑕᐅᑉ ᑕᑉ ᖄᒃᒍ ᐃᑎᐱᐊᓂᒥᐅᑕᓐᑦ ᐊᕐ ᓄᐊᕐ ᑭᑐᑦ
ᐊᒍ ᑕᓗ ᑕᕐᖅᐱᐊᓂᒥᑐᑦ ᐳᐃᖅᕐᖅᕐ ᑎᐅᖃᑐᕐᑦ, ᑐᑯᕐᖅᕐ ᑎᑎᐊ
ᐊᒍ ᓇᑉᕐ ᓂᐊᕐᖅᑉ.

ᐅᒪᔨᕐ ᓂᐊᓂᖅᕐ ᑕᐃᒪᑦᑲᖅᕐ ᕐᖅᕐ ᒪᑐᔅ ᑎᑉᕐ ᕐᒍ ᐱᑎᐊᑐᕐᕐᖅᕐ
ᑕᑯᓯᑦ ᐃᓄᐅᑦ. ᓂᖅᒥᑐ ᐊᐃᕐ ᕐᕐᖅᕐ. ᑐᕐᕐᒪᖅᕐᒍᑦ ᓄᐊᕐᖅ
ᐊᒍ ᐅᒪᔨᖅᕐ ᐊᕐᐊᓄᕐᒍᑎᑐᖅᕐ ᐊᖅᓄᕐ ᑐᖅᕐ, ᐊᒍ ᐱᑎᓇᕐᖅᕐᖅᕐ
ᑕᑯᓯᑦ ᐃᓄᐅᑦ ᑕᑕᐊ ᒪᑭ ᖅᕐ ᕐᖅ ᖃᐅᔨᑦᕐᓇᒪᖅᕐ ᐃᓄᕐᖅᖅᕐᖅᕐ.

It was not always so. There were times before when
we would not have food for the winter. Many people were
starving in the Village. One time six or seven people died
here. But I was not afraid. I told my father I would find food
for the Village.

I waited at the edge of the ice for three days looking for
the whale. He saw me and came close enough for me to kill
him with my harpoon. He was heavy but I pulled him up
onto the ice. I gave my family the largest share. My father
was very proud. He told me, 'To be so young and yet to have
killed the great one from the sea. You are a great hunter.'
Everyone was very happy. And we sang and danced and ate
the whale until we were all tired.

ᶜCᐃLᐊᒍˢᒥᖅ ᔨᕐᓴᔨᒪˢᒥᒍᖅ. ᐊᒥ ᔨᐊᔅ ᔨC Cᐃᒥᔨᒪᓯ ᐅᖁᐅᔾᑎᒪᓯᒍ
ᓂᖅᕎᖅᕥᒧᔨᒪᔨᖢᑦᐸ. ᐊᒥᔨᐊᓘᐊᔅ ᐃᓂᐃᔅ ᐱᔅ ᔨᑎᓐᖃ ᓂᐅᒥᓂ
ᑐᔨᐊᖅᕤᓚᒥᒪᔅ. Cᐃᔅ ᔨᒪᓂᒥᐊᖅᖧ ᐱᓯᔨᐊᔅ ᓱᖃ ᔨᐃᑲ ᑐᐊᒥ Ꮢᓱᓂᖢ
Cᒪ ᓄᐊᒥᓄ ᑐᔨᔨᒪᔨᔅ. ᖀᔨᐊᓄ ᑲᐱᐊᔨᒪᔅᒥᒍᔮ.
ᐆᖀᐅᖃ ᐱᒥᐅᑦ ᔨᒪᔨᔮ ᐊᒧᒪᓂ ᓄᐊᒥᓄᖃ ᓂᖅᑖ ᓴᔨᐅᒥᐅᔨᖅᕤᔨ ᔨᔮᓟ.'

'ᐅᒍᖅᕡᑈ ᔨᒪᔨᔮ ᔨᓇˢ ᔨᐊᓄ ᐱᓯᔨᖢᖃ ᐅᔅᓄᖃ ᖀᐱᒧᓯ ᔨᐅᔨᓟ.
ᐆᔨᓄ Cᔨᔨᖃ ᖃᑲᓐᒪCᐅᔅ ᔨᒪᔨᖅᕙ ᐊᐅᒪᐃᔨᓂᔨᖅᕥᓄᖢᒍ ᑐᔨᔨᒪᑲᐅᔅ ᔨᒪᖅᕥ.
ᐅᔨᖢᒪᐊᒍᐊᔨᐅᖢᐊᔨᔅ ᓐᔮᒍ ᔨᔅᑈ ᖃᔅᐅᒪᔅ ᖃᖄ ᐊᓐᒥᐅᔅ ᔨᒪᖅᕥ. ᐃᒥᖃ
ᐊᔅᔮᓄᔅ ᔨᐸᖃ ᓂᔅᓗᖃ ᓐᒥᐅᔅ ᔨᒪᖅᕤ. ᐊᑈᒪ ᐱᐊᔨᐃᖢᐱᐊᔾᓱᐅᔅ ᔨᒪᔨᖃ.
ᐆᖂᐅᔅ ᐅᖃᕡᐅᔅ ᔨᒪᔨᖅᕙ, 'ᐃᓂᔾᑐᐊᐱᐅᔅ ᔨᓐᓯ ᐅᔨᔨᖃᐊᔅ ᐃᓗᔅ ᒥᐅ-
ᒥᔅ ᔨᐊᖁᔨᖅᕝ, ᐅᓟᔨᖅᕜ ᔨᐅᓐᒥᔨᐊᔿᔨᓐᔅ.' ᐃᔨᐊᓐᖅᕙ ᐃᓂᖅᕥᓐᖅᕙ
ᖅᕶᐊᐊᔾᔨᖢᓐᐊᔿᐅᔅ ᔨᒪᔨᔅ. ᐃᔅᔮᑈᔿ ᐊᒥᔮ Cᓄᔨᔅ ᔿC ᖃᒪᔨᖢ-
ᒥᐊᓄᔅᒥᖅᕝ ᓂᓐᒥᐊᐅᔅ ᔨᒪᔨᔾ ᑈᖃᖃᖅᕙᔅ ᔿC.'

We don't use dogs anymore to pull the Kmotik (sled). We still use them for their fur for our parkas. In the past when a village was starving we would have to eat the dogs. Now, we have the Ski-doo to take us great distances for hunting. But if you become lost, or run out of gas, or there are no animals to kill, you cannot eat your Ski-doo. It seems that we have lost more than we have gained.

ᕿᕐᒥᓇᖅ ᐊᒍᔅ ᐸᒐᐃᑐᒍᖅ, ᕿᒍᖅ ᓯᑎᑎᕆᐯᒐᐃᑎᖕ. ᓄᐃᓕᑎᐸᑏᓇᖕᖑᐊᖅ ᓯᖕᒃ ᒥᕐᖕᕆᖅ. ᑕᐃᖅ ᓯᒐᓗᖕ ᓄᓇᖕᖅ ᐱᖕᓕᐊᓗᓗᑐᐊᖕᒥᖕ ᓂᑎᐸᖕᕃ ᐸᒐᐃᖅ ᑐᒍᖕ ᕿᕐᒥᓇᖕ. ᒪᓇᖕ, ᓯᕿᑐᖕᕃ ᐸᓗᐊᒍᒍᖕ ᕿᖕᖕᑎᑐᐊᓗᒍᖕ ᐊᐃᓇᑎᑐᒍᓇᐸᓯᖕ ᒃᖕᒃ ᒪᖕᖕᐊᒃᑐᐊᖕᒃ. ᐱᖕᐊᓄ ᐊᖕᐸᒍᖕᖕ, ᐅᐸᓄᖕ ᐅᖕ ᓯᐊᐱᖕᖕ, ᐅᐸᓄᖕ ᐅᒪᖕᖕᕿᖕᖕᐸᖕ ᑐᖕᒪᖕᖕ ᕚᒥᖕ, ᒪᖕ ᓯᕿᑐᖕᕃ ᓂᖕᕃᖕᐸᖕᒃᑕᐃᖕ. ᐊᐸᐅᖕᓕᐸᖕᕃᐯᖕ ᐊᒥᖕᓇᖕ ᕼᐊᐯᖕᖕ ᑐᖕ ᐸᑎᖕᓕᐸᖕᕃᖕᐸᓄᖕ.'

When we are hunting we do not look for the animal, but a movement, a disturbance, an interruption in the rhythm of the land.

‘ᐅᒪᔪᕐ ᓯᐅᓕᑐᐊᕋᑕ ᑕᓇ ᐅᒪᔪᖅ ᕿᓂᓱᕐᑐᑦᔭᕐᒋᑕᕗᑦ, ᑭᓯᐊᓂᓕ ᐊᐅᓚᑦᔭᑐᒥᒃ, ᓂᒪᒐᓚᑐᒥᒃ, ᐊᓯᑦᐳᔪᒥᒃ ᓄᓇᐅᑉ ᐱᐅᓯᕐᒐᓂᒃ ᕿᓂᓱᕐᑐᕗᑐᑦ.’

All unexpected I came upon and took by surprise the heed-less dweller of the plains. . . .

ˁσ∩ᗡΓᐳᗡᶜ ᐳᴀˁL ∩ᑭᗡ∩ᒐᗡˁ ᐳˢL ᐊLᒡ ˁᖁᐊˁ ᑫ∩ᶜ ᕊᒍ Cᴀ
ᖲˢΓᕊᐊˢᒋᒍˢᵇ ᴀ∩ˢ ᴀΓᗡCˢᵇ. . . .ˀ

The way we live right now, by hunting, is going to be lost in the future. The memories of the past are going to disappear. But if we try hard enough, if we try to teach our children, I hope maybe we are not going to forget.

‘ᒪᓇ ᐃᓅᓯᑎᓴᕗᑦ, ᐅᒪᔪᕐ ᓯᐅᓂᖅ, ᓯᕗᓂᑎᓂ ᐊᓯᐅᓚᕐᒐᔪᖅ.
ᑕᒪᑯᐊ ᑕᐃᑦ ᓯᒪᓂᑕᐃᑦ ᐊᐅᓚᕆᓴᕗᑦ ᓅᐃᑕᒍᓇᐃᓚᕐᒐᔪᑦ.
ᑭᓯᐊᓂ ᐊᑦ ᓯᕈᓗᑕ ᐱᒐᓯᐊᑦ ᓯᐊᕈᑕ, ᐃᓕᓂᐊᑎᑦ ᓯᒐᓯᐊᕈᑕ
ᕐᑭᑐᖅ ᕐᒐᑎᓂᒃ, ᐃᒪᖅᑲ ᐳᐃᒍᓚᕐᒐᕐᒥᑲᓗᐊᖅ ᑐᒍᑦ.’

From a distance it looked like a man. As we came closer on the Ski-doo I saw that it was in fact what the Inuit call an Inukshuk. It stood there like a sentinel.

The 'people rock' or 'spirit rock,' a symbol of the past, is now only a directional marker.

I once read that the Inukshuk used to appear more human, sometimes with armlike appendages. It was created to make the desolate land appear inhabited. A reminder of Spirit to both Man and Animal.

I only heard the word Inukshuk mentioned twice in the Inuit vocabulary. It is something that has passed out of their culture.

ᖃᓂᕐᒥᑐᑦ ᓱᓂ ᐊᕐᔪᑎᕐ ᐹᔭᕐ ᑐᖅ. ᓯᑭᑐᑯᑦ ᖃᓂᓕᐸᓕᐊᓕᖁᑎᔪ ᓱᓇᐅᕙ ᐃᓄᑐᐃᓇᐃᑦ ᐃᓄᑦ ᓱᓂᖁᕐ ᑕᕐᒪᑦ. ᑕᐃᑲᓂ ᓂᑯᕐ ᖁᔮᖅ ᐸᐃᕐ ᓯᔮᑎᑐᑦ (ᐅᓇᑕᕐ ᑎᑎᑐᑦ).

'ᐅᔭᖁᖅ ᐃᓄᔭᕐ ᑐᖅ' ᐅᕙᓗᓂᑦ 'ᐊᓂᕐ ᓂᓕᒃ ᐅᔭᖁᖅ,' ᓄᐃᑕᑎᑦ ᓯᔮᖅ ᑕᐃᑦ ᓱᒪᓂᑕᕐ ᒥᒃ, ᒪᓇᐅᓕᕐ ᑐᖅ ᑕᒪᑎᑯᑎᑐᐃᓇᐅᓕᖁᖅ.

ᐊᑐᐊᕐᓯᓚᐅᕐ ᓯᒪᒥᒪᒪ ᐃᓄᑦ ᓱᐃᔪᖅ ᑕᐃᑦ ᓱᒪᓂ ᐃᓄᑐᐊᓗᔭᕐ ᐸᓂᕐ ᒪᑕ, ᐃᓕᕐᒪᓂᐊᓕᑦ ᑕᓕᕐᔪᐊᖅᑲᕐ ᐸᓱᑎᒃ. ᓴᓇᔭᐅᓯᒪᔮᖅ ᑕᒪᓇ ᓄᓇᑐᐃᓇᓗᒃ ᓱᓇᖅᑲᕐᒥᑐᖅ ᐃᓄᑕᓕᕐ ᔮᔭᕐ ᑎᒪᓱᐊᓗᑦ. ᐃᖅᑲᐅᒪᔪᑎᑦ ᓴᕐᒪ ᐃᓄᑉ ᐅᒪᔮᓗ ᐊᓂᕐ ᓂᒥᒃ.

ᑕᓇ ᐃᓄᑦ ᓱᖅ ᐅᖅᑲᕐ ᑕᐅᑎᓗᔪ ᐃᓄᓄᑦ ᒪᒃ ᕿᑲᑐᐃᓇᓱᔪ ᑐᓴᓚᐅᔭᖁ. ᑕᓇ ᐃᓕᖅᑯᓯᕐᒪᓂ ᐊᓂᔪᕐ ᓯᒪᓕᕐ ᑐᖅ.

IN THE MIDDLE

has been set in a film version of Trump Medieval, a typeface designed by Professor Georg Trump in the mid-1950s and cast by the C. E. Weber Typefoundry of Stuttgart, West Germany. The roman letter forms of Trump Medieval are based on classical prototypes, but have been interpreted by Professor Trump in a distinctly modern style. The italic letter forms are more of a sloped roman than a true italic in design, a characteristic shared by many contemporary type-faces. The result is a modern and distinguished type, notable both for its legibility and versatility.

The text was composed by Roy McCoy and printed by Rembrandt Press, Milford, Connecticut, on Warren's 80# Lustre White Dull, an entirely acid-free paper. The photographs were shot with a 250-line screen and printed in duo-tone. Robert Burlen & Son, Hingham, Massachusetts was the bindery.

The book was designed by Katie Homans. Inuit syllabics by Kathleen Borowik, title page calligraphy by Renée Cossutta, and map by Jacqueline Sakwa.

Endpaper drawings are by Anarqaq, an Inuit shaman. These dream visions appeared to him while he sat for long periods in silent concentration.